Playback:

The Story of
Recording Devices

Playback:
The Story of Recording Devices

By ROBERT K. KRISHEF

Illustrated by GEORGE OVERLIE

Prepared under the supervision of Robert W. Surplus

Musical Books for Young People

LERNER PUBLICATIONS COMPANY
MINNEAPOLIS, MINNESOTA

International Copyright Secured. Printed in U.S.A.

Library of Congress Catalog Card Number: 62-18817

Second Printing 1963
Third Printing 1964
Fourth Printing 1965
Fifth Printing 1967

Contents

Listening to Music

Did you know that music is written and played for you? Well, it isn't <u>just</u> for you, of course. Music is really for <u>us</u>— for you and me, and everyone who enjoys listening to it.

A painter hangs his finished picture in an art gallery so everyone can look at it. An author wants his book in a store or library so everyone can read it. The great composers did not create only for themselves, but also for those who would hear their music.

Music has always attracted audiences. Musicians performed in the dim light of a campfire and in the splendor of a king's court. Long ago, some men even earned their living as singing storytellers. They were called minstrels.

In those days, of course, there were no movies to attend, television shows to watch, or magazines to read. Listening to minstrels was one of the few ways of being entertained. So people were glad when a minstrel came along with his harp to play and sing for them.

Although music has always been popular, it has never been more popular than it is today. This is because more people are now able to enjoy music.

Only a few hundred people could listen to the minstrel in the king's court. In the United States in the 19th century, larger cities such as New York, Boston, and Chicago built concert halls and organized fine symphony orchestras. But only a few thousand could attend a concert at any one time. Today, however, many millions of people enjoy music right in their own homes. Record players and tape recorders are the devices they use.

How has all this happened? Let's take a look at some of the people and ideas that have made this possible.

What Is Sound?

The first recording device was invented by Thomas Edison in 1877. He called his invention the *phonograph*. The name comes from two Greek words—*phono* means sound, and *graph* means writing.

To understand how sound can be written or recorded on a record or tape, we must understand some things about sound itself.

The sounds we hear are vibrations in the air. Sound vibrations are something like the wind. We cannot see it, but we can feel it. We cannot see sound vibrations either, but our eardrums can feel them, and we can hear them.

Imagine silence as a straight line: ——————————— When you speak or sing, the straight line becomes wavy with vibrations: /\/\/\/\/\ . We say that vibrations form *sound waves*.

When you hear a sound, you describe it in two ways: (1) the sound is either loud or soft, (2) the sound is either high or low.

The loudness and softness is called *amplitude*. Here is a loud sound: \/\/\/\/\ . Notice how high the waves are. Here is a soft sound: /\/\/\/\/\ . The waves are not as high. You can see that more air is put in motion with a loud sound than with a soft sound. The more air in motion, the greater the amplitude.

The number of vibrations, or *frequency,* makes a sound high or low. Here is a high sound: /\/\/\/\/\/\/\/\ . Notice how close together the waves are. These waves move very quickly. Here is a low sound: /\/\/\/\ . These waves are farther apart. They move more slowly.

The human ear can hear sounds from about 20 to 20,000 vibrations per second. Not every one can hear all these sounds. If there are too few vibrations, or too many, we cannot hear the sound. This is why we can hear a bee, but not a butterfly. A butterfly's wings do not cause enough vibrations of air per second to make a sound. A bee's wings do. An example of noise that is too high, or that has too many vibrations for the human ear, is the sound made by a special dog whistle. Dogs can hear much higher sounds than people.

Thomas Edison knew that sound is made by vibrations moving through the air. Edison used this knowledge while working on improvements for the telephone, which had been invented in 1876 by Alexander Graham Bell.

He could not judge the amplitude of the sounds he heard over the telephone because he was partly deaf. So he attached a needle to the telephone receiver. Holding his finger against the needle, he was able to feel the vibrations whenever sound caused the receiver and the needle to vibrate.

Another invention Edison was working on was the telegraph. He wanted to take a telegraph message at one speed and send it out at a faster speed. He punched out the dots and dashes of Morse code on a paper tape. Then he ran the tape through a machine he had built to send messages at different speeds. As he did this, he noticed a strange sound that was very much like the human voice.

Edison saw that there was a connection between his experiences with the telephone and telegraph. He reasoned that if sounds could make a needle vibrate to scratch his finger, then a needle could also be used to store the sounds of the human voice on a paper tape. Later the tape could be played back. These thoughts led to the first sound recording device.

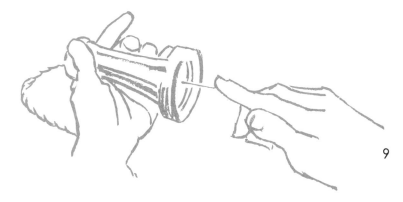

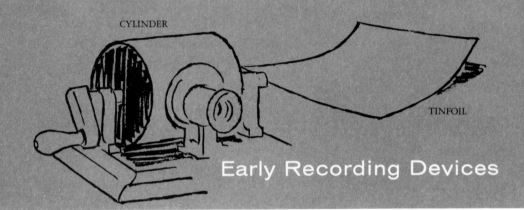

CYLINDER

TINFOIL

Early Recording Devices

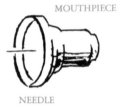

MOUTHPIECE

NEEDLE

Edison's first phonograph was very simple. A cylinder was covered with tin foil and attached to a screw. A needle was fastened to a metal plate on the mouthpiece and rested against the cylinder. When people spoke or sang into the mouthpiece, the sound waves from their voices caused both the metal plate and needle to vibrate. The cylinder was turned by a handle connected to the screw, and the vibrating needle pressed the sound into the tin foil.

Edison called his recordings *phonograms,* which means "sound that is written." The first phonogram was made when he shouted "Mary had a little lamb" into the mouthpiece. Can you imagine how excited he must have been

when he played the recording back, and heard his own voice for the first time from a machine?

The sound was very poor, of course, compared with the records of today. It was probably like the sound of "talking" birthday cards that wish you "happy birthday", or like dolls that speak. Even this was remarkable at that time. People were amazed with the phonograph, just as they were with the first automobile and first airplane.

Although people were fascinated with the phonograph, it did not remain popular for very long. Not only was the sound bad, but the tin foil wore out too quickly. Nothing at all could be heard after the recording was played about six times.

Meanwhile, Edison was busy with experiments that were to lead to the electric light bulb. This took all of his interest and time. For a few years, nothing much happened to his idea of a tin foil record and a hand-cranked phonograph.

Then two men, Chichester Bell and Charles Tainter, developed a new phonograph which they called the *graphophone*. Can you guess where they got that name? Graphophone is phonograph turned around!

GRAPHOPHONE

In 1881, they placed a box with a graphophone cylinder in the Smithsonian Institution in Washington. In 1937, the box was opened, and the cylinder played. The message said in part: "G-r-r, I am a graphophone, and my mother was a phonograph."

The graphophone was better than the phonograph. Instead of a tin foil cylinder, sound was recorded on a cylinder of cardboard covered with a thin coating of hard wax. Although earphones were needed to hear the recording properly, the sound was much more like the sound sung or played into the mouthpiece than was possible with Edison's phonograph.

When Edison finished his work on the electric light bulb in 1887, he turned his attention once again to the phonograph he had invented ten years before. His new phonograph looked a great deal like the graphophone. However, he made one important change. His records were made of solid wax, rather than wax-covered cardboard. This meant that grooves made by the needle could be scraped off, and new sounds recorded on the same wax cylinder.

By this time, motors powered by heavy-duty batteries were being used to turn the cylinders of some phonographs and graphophones. Motors worked much better than the hand crank of the first phonograph and the foot peddles used to operate early graphophones. The motor turned the cylinder at an even speed. This improved the sound.

The improved sound interested musicians. They wanted people to hear their music and, of course, they were anxious to hear it themselves!

It is reported that a strange thing happened when Hans von Bülow, a German pianist and conductor, made his first record. When he heard the playback, he

HEAVY-DUTY BATTERY

13

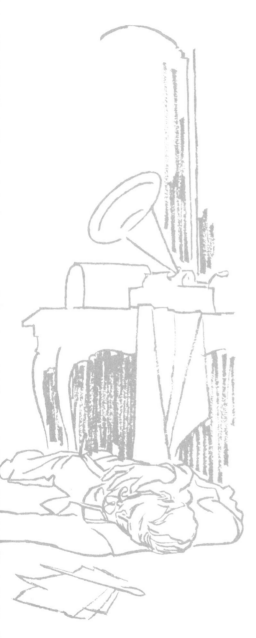

fainted, perhaps in astonishment at listening to himself play.

The von Bülow cylinder, like so many other early records, has never been found. Collectors are still searching for it. Maybe some day one of them will find this very important record.

If you saw a phonograph from those days, the first thing to catch your eye would be the large horn to which the needle was fastened. Sounds were heard through this horn. You can see for yourself what it was like to hear a record that way. Select an old record of little value—one you don't want anymore. Make a sheet of paper into a shape like an ice cream cone. Hold a needle or pin inside the cone, and push it down through the pointed end. Place the old record on your phonograph, and put the needle in the record groove. Play the record, and you will hear it through the open part of your paper cone.

By the 1890's, companies were making records for sale to the public. A great favorite was the United States Marine Band conducted by John Philip Sousa. Sousa was known as the "March King", and his big seller was *Semper Fidelis*.

A band or orchestra recording session in those days was very interesting. The musicians were placed very close together. The first row of musicians sat on low stools, and the second row on higher stools. The third row stood, and the fourth row climbed on tables or platforms. The musicians faced ten large horns. Each horn was connected to a needle and a phonograph.

When all ten phonographs were going, the band started playing, and each needle made a recording on a wax cylinder. Then new cylinders were put in and ten more recordings were made, and then ten more, and so on. You can see that it took a long time to make a lot of records. John Philip Sousa and his band must have gotten very tired of playing *Semper Fidelis* over and over again!

Advancement in the
Phonograph Industry

Although Edison was the first to build a phonograph, a man named Emile Berliner could be considered the "father of the modern phonograph." He called his machine the *gramophone*. If you remember how the term graphophone was adapted from phonograph, then you can guess where the name gramophone came from (Edison called his recordings phonograms).

Berliner introduced several ideas still in use today. First of all, his needle made lateral, or side-to-side, cuts in the wax instead of the up-and-down cuts which had been made by earlier recording devices. The lateral method is used in recording today. Second, instead of records like cylinders, Berliner's records were flat. These records were very much like the records of today. A third idea, which was probably Berliner's most important, was his way of making records from a single *master record*.

For recording, he used a zinc disc covered with a special wax. After the vibrating needle made its grooves in the wax, the disc was dropped into acid. The special wax protected the disc, except where the wax had been cut away by the needle. Here the acid ate into the zinc, and left grooves in the metal.

Next, Berliner covered the zinc disc with a thin layer of nickel and copper. When that covering was removed, it was also a disc—a reverse of the master record.

You have had pictures taken of yourself, haven't you? Suppose you are holding a ball in your right hand when the picture is taken. When the film is developed, it becomes a "negative," meaning that everything is reversed. On this negative, the ball is in your left hand. When the negative is printed on photo paper, you have a "true" picture, and the ball is in your right hand.

In the same way, Berliner took this reverse record and pressed it out on another kind of material. The result was a copy of the original zinc disc. Just as any number of prints can be made from a negative, so could a great many records be made from that one reverse record.

Berliner experimented with several materials from which to press records. Finally, he tried a plastic used in making buttons. This material worked very well. It was very much like the shellac used in making billions of records after that.

The gramophone had a better motor than the phonograph or graphophone. Its motor was like a sewing machine motor. Eldridge Johnson, a mechanic who worked for Berliner, was responsible for this improvement. Later, when Johnson had his own company, he developed a method of using a wax disc as a master record.

Johnson also introduced the most famous of all phonographs— the *Victrola*. People the age of your grandparents possibly recall the Victrola very well. Ask them. Sometimes a person says "Victrola", the name of just one particular phonograph, when he is talking about phonographs in general.

The Victrola was the first talking machine which really looked like a piece of living room furniture. The horn, which sent out the sound waves, was bent over and put inside a cabinet. The Victrola had a flat lid, so that flowers, pictures, or books could be kept on it when records were not being played.

While progress was being made in the phonograph industry people's love for music continued to grow. Thousands were attending symphonies in the great new concert halls that had been built in our large cities. Pupils were learning to sing in school, as well as learning reading, writing, and arithmetic. School choirs, bands, and orchestras were being formed. Also, symphony orchestra conductors thought of giving concerts just for young people, so that they could learn more about music.

But the phonograph had made possible the most wonderful idea of all! Frances Elliott Clark, a music teacher in Milwaukee, brought a phonograph into her classrooms. Instead of just talking about music, she taught it by playing records. She was so successful that other teachers did the same thing. Soon young people from small country schools could be as familiar with music as those from large cities who were attending concerts.

People also began to use records for dancing. Sales of dance records rose as the phonograph became an ideal instrument for home entertainment. Those who had never bought records before started buying them for parties.

The phonograph industry was "big business." In 1914, there were 18 manufacturers producing 500,000 phonographs. By 1919, there were nearly 200 manufacturers making more than two million phonographs. The time from 1907 to 1924 is sometimes called the "golden age of recording." It is said that there were as many records sold in those years as in the next 35 years combined.

For a time during the 1930's, the phonograph slipped in popularity. It was replaced by the radio for home music and entertainment. Music over the radio was free, and this was important at that time. There was a depression in the United States. Many people were out of work or had their salaries reduced.

But later, things improved. Soon record companies put coin phonographs called "juke boxes" in drug stores and restaurants. People heard records on the juke boxes and over the radio and began to buy them again.

The records they were buying were better than ever. The phonograph industry had found an exciting new way to make records. This new method was electrical recording. The use of electricity to record sounds completely changed the world of the phonograph. It began the modern era of sound recording—the era which we are in today.

The Microphone Replaces the Recording Horn

You remember that sound is produced by vibrations, and that our ears can hear sounds from about 20 to 20,000 vibrations per second. Early records, made from music played into the old recording horn, had a range of only about 168 to 2,000 vibrations. Therefore, a note causing more than 2,000 vibrations or a note creating less than 168 vibrations was not too accurately recorded.

You also know that a sound, in addition to being high or low, is described

by its amplitude (loudness or softness). Bands used to stand close together in front of the recording horn. It was the amplitude, or the force of the sound waves coming through the recording horn, that caused the needle to cut grooves in a record. In those days, the best records were made from music that was very loud.

Sounds from any distance are now picked up easily by electrical recording. The microphone has replaced the recording horn. Have you ever heard someone speak or sing into a microphone? The sound coming from the microphone is much louder than the person's voice. Sometimes a microphone may stop working while a person is singing or talking —then you really can tell the difference in amplitude.

However, the microphone itself does not make sounds louder. The microphone changes sound waves into electrical signals. Loud notes send more electricity than soft notes. High notes, with their rapid vibrations of air, send rapid bursts of electricity over the microphone. There is more space between vibrations of a low note, and more space between the bursts of electricity.

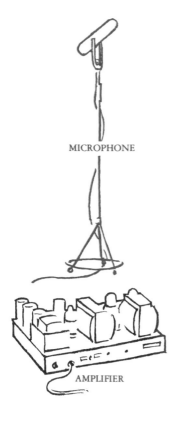

MICROPHONE

AMPLIFIER

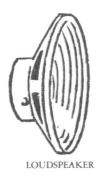

LOUDSPEAKER

The pattern of electrical signals is like a tiny snapshot. The snapshot has details that the camera recorded when the picture was taken. However, the snapshot has to be enlarged for you to see the details clearly.

In the same way, the electrical signals fit the pattern of the sound waves. A note of 440 vibrations per second is changed into 440 electrical signals per second, a note of 880 vibrations into 880 signals. But the pattern from the microphone is very small, because the microphone gives very little current. It is necessary to enlarge, or *amplify,* this current.

The job of strengthening the electrical current is done by an instrument called the *amplifier.* After the electrical signals are enlarged, they are sent through a loudspeaker, which changes them back into sound waves. It is this teamwork of microphone-amplifier-loudspeaker that makes sound loud enough to hear when you are sitting far away from the speaker in an auditorium or theater.

Although there are various types of microphones, they all operate on the same general idea. They change the original sound waves to signals of electrical current.

Microphones "hear" in different ways. Some pick up only sounds in front, and some pick up sounds in front and back, but not from the sides. Others can hear sounds from all sides. A recording can be made with one microphone. It can be made with several microphones of the same type. It can also be made with several microphones of different types.

The way microphones are used to make recordings is extremely important. A recording engineer must know what kinds of microphones to use, how many, and where to place them. He must consider the type of studio or auditorium in which the recording is being made. He must know what microphone arrangement is best for a band, for a soloist, or for a symphony orchestra. He has many problems to solve in order to get the best recording possible.

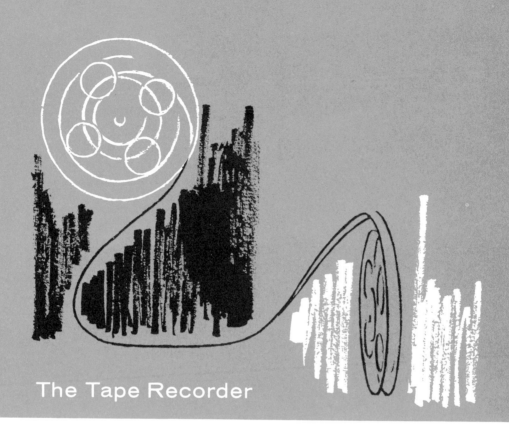

The Tape Recorder

Until recent years, the story of recording devices was mainly about the development of various types of record players— phonographs, graphophones, and gramophones. In the modern era of sound recording, the tape recorder has become extremely important. It is used in the manufacture of records, and as a home playback unit.

The tape recorder was invented in 1899 by a Danish engineer, Vladimir Poulsen. It was not widely used for a long time, since it did not record as clearly as a phonograph.

Magnetic recording finally became popular during World War II. Important meetings and conferences were recorded on steel tape. Also, German scientists developed an advanced type of recorder, the *magnetophone*. This instrument used plastic tape coated with iron oxide. It recorded sounds up to 10,000 vibrations, equaling the finest phonograph records then in use. But the magnetophone required heavy equipment and large reels, and was not practical for home use.

In the United States, recordings were made on stainless steel wire. Wire recorders were popular for only a short time because they did not provide satisfactory sound. Wire is still used when quality sound is not necessary, as in some dictating machines.

In 1947, a magnetic tape was introduced with a new type of iron oxide coating far better than what the Germans used. This tape recorded up to 15,000 vibrations, and its reel was much smaller than the magnetophone's.

Do you know how a tape recorder works? It changes the pattern of electrical current from a microphone into a magnetic pattern on tape. Magnetic tape is a quarter-inch wide strip of plastic, coated with millions of very tiny specks of *iron oxide*. In recording, these specks are arranged in patterns by a device called an *electromagnet*.

An electromagnet is a piece of iron with wire wrapped around it, and with electric current flowing through that wire. The current is an electrical signal from the sound wave. The pattern which the electromagnet arranges on tape is made from signals from the current. This means that the magnetic tape has the same pattern as the original sound wave.

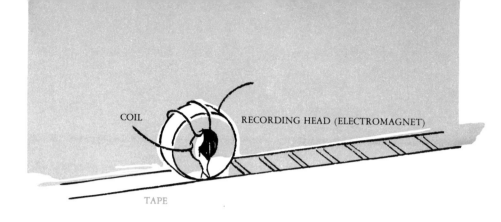

COIL   RECORDING HEAD (ELECTROMAGNET)

TAPE

A tape recorder has three electromagnets. The first, called the *erase head,* mixes up the iron oxide particles. When you erase chalk from a blackboard, there is nothing left to show what was on the board—if you did a good job. Well, this first electromagnet <u>does</u> do a good job. By mixing up the iron oxide particles, it erases any pattern that was recorded before.

The second electromagnet is the one that records the electrical pattern from the microphone. This pattern is stored on the tape, and can be played back whenever needed.

The third electromagnet is for playing back the recording. Here, the opposite of magnetic recording takes place. Instead of current in the electromagnet magnetizing the tape, the magnetic tape creates a current in the electromagnet. This current is amplified, sent through a loudspeaker, and changed to the sound waves which we hear.

Today many tapes with music on them are sold for home use. A single tape can provide almost two hours of music. Owners of tape recorders sometimes use them to record directly from radio and television programs. Tape does not wear out. Sound on the tape can be erased, and the same tape used again and again. These are some of the reasons why people like to use the tape recorder in their homes.

The Record and Record Player Today

Today, we call records *high fidelity* or *hi-fi* for short. This means that the sound we hear from our record player is as close as possible to the sound of an orchestra in the concert hall.

Hi-fi, like tape recording, got its big start during World War II. But this time it was the English, and not the Germans, who made this important advancement.

An English record company was asked to make a record to show the difference in sound between English and German submarines. The armed forces planned to use this record in training their men. The differences in sound between these two types of submarines could not be clearly recorded or heard on the equipment then in use. It was necessary to find new ways of recording and playing back the sounds.

When the war was over, these improvements were used to record music. When English records began to come to the United States after the war, every-

one was amazed at how lifelike they were. People said that when they listened to them, it was almost as if they were in the same room as the orchestra.

In 1947, when modern magnetic tape was introduced, the phonograph record was still old-fashioned. It was no different in size, playing time, and grooving from what it had been in 1903. Manufacturers thought a record had to be made and played back at 78 RPM (revolutions per minute). A *revolution* is the full-circle spin made by the *turntable*. The turntable is the flat plate on which the record is placed. The 78 (or to be exact, 78.26) RPM records had a playing time of about four minutes.

For years scientists tried to add more playing time to records. In 1948, records were finally developed that revolved at slower speeds with no loss in quality. Today we have LP (long playing) records which make only 33⅓ or 45 revolutions per minute. There are even some 16⅔ RPM records.

To add even more playing time, record grooves were moved closer together. Most old records had about 100 grooves to an inch.

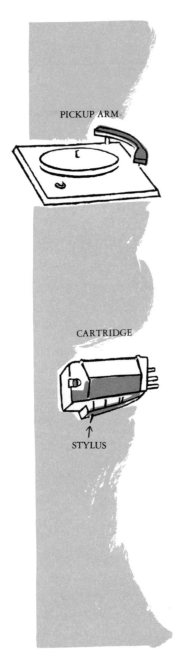

PICKUP ARM

CARTRIDGE

STYLUS

The new ones, called micro-groove records, have about fifty minutes of music—still less than tape, but enough to make records very enjoyable.

Because the grooves in long playing records are smaller and closer together, these records must be played with a needle which has a very small, perfectly-formed tip. Some record players come with two needles, one for 78 RPM records and one for LP's.

The needle, or *stylus* as it is known, is set in a little box called the *cartridge* or *pickup*. The cartridge is attached to the *pickup arm*.

As the record turns, the stylus rides in the grooves, picking up the vibrations of sound. A stylus works properly when it rides in the grooves in such a way that the clearest and truest sound is picked up with the least wear on the record. The old-fashioned needle was made of steel, wood, or thorn. Today the best and longest-lasting stylus is made of diamond. Others are made of ruby or sapphire.

Vibrations from the stylus create an electrical current in the cartridge. The cartridge sends the current to the ampli-

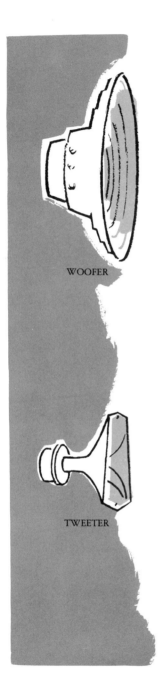

WOOFER

TWEETER

fier. The accuracy of the current depends not only on a good stylus and cartridge, but also on the quality of the pickup arm. A poor arm, that is too heavy or not well-balanced, will *distort,* or change the sound.

The electrical current changes as the sounds picked up by the stylus change. High notes are turned into rapid electrical signals by the cartridge. Low notes make signals farther apart.

After the current is strengthened by the amplifier, it is sent into the loudspeaker of your record player. The loudspeaker, remember, changes the electrical signals into sound waves which we hear.

Most record players have what are called *woofer* and *tweeter* speakers. The woofer is specially made to receive and send out the slow, wide vibrations of low notes. The tweeter is a smaller speaker made for the fast, short vibrations of high notes.

A separating device sends high pitch notes to the tweeter and low pitch notes to the woofer. Sometimes the two are combined in one speaker where the tweeter is mounted within the woofer. This is called a *coaxial* speaker.

Modern Record Making

Record making today is far different than it was at the turn of the century. Sousa's men would be amazed at how easy it is, compared to what they went through.

This is how records are made today. First, the sound from the microphone is recorded on tape. There are several reasons for this. Tape can be played back immediately. The tape is merely rewound and sent past the playback head. If a mistake is made, it is easy to make changes or corrections. Instead of recording an entire selection over again, it is necessary to record only the part to be improved. The poor part is cut out, and the new part put in its place. This is called *splicing* the tape.

Almost every tape is spliced in one place or another, because a recording is seldom made without at least one mistake. When splicing is done by an expert, it is impossible to tell where the tape has been cut and put together again. Even one wrong note can be corrected on tape.

The recording studio sends the finished tape to the factory. A master record is made by playing the tape. The sound from the tape causes the needle to vibrate, cutting the original sound waves into the master record.

This master record is made of aluminum with a smooth layer of shiny black lacquer as a cast. Several negatives, called *pressers,* are made from the master record, and are used to turn out finished records—the same idea introduced by Emile Berliner in 1887.

Today, records are made in a record press, something like the way waffles are made in a waffle iron. The waffles are shaped by the pattern on the top and bottom of the waffle iron. In making a record, two pressers with different recording patterns are placed on the top and on the bottom of the press. Both sides of the record are then made at the same time.

The material used for records is vinylite, a plastic. The record press is steam-heated to a temperature of 300 degrees. The heat melts the vinylite so that it fits the pattern of the grooves on the pressers. Cold water then replaces the steam, and hardens the record.

In this way, music is "packaged" or "stored" on a record. It is like a package of fresh frozen strawberries, or other good things to eat that you see in a supermarket. These strawberries are picked, and preserved until they are unpackaged and defrosted for use in your home. Music is taken out of its package when your phonograph picks up the sound from the grooves of the record.

High Fidelity and Stereo

Today we have fine records and tapes, and fine equipment on which to play them. This combination gives us high fidelity sound—music as close as possible to the sound heard in the studio.

Some people get confused about the terms *high fidelity* and *stereophonic* and think they mean the same thing. This is a mistake, because they do not. With high fidelity equipment, we can hear music much closer to the sound heard in the concert hall, than we could with the equipment of ten or twenty years ago. We can also hear more clearly just how

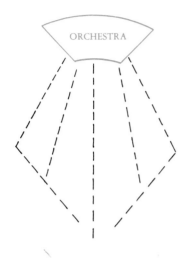

ORCHESTRA

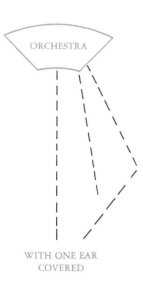

ORCHESTRA

WITH ONE EAR
COVERED

the different instruments sound. Stereophonic, or *stereo* for short, is a word to describe a new way of listening to recorded music.

To understand how stereo makes music more enjoyable, let us first imagine that we are in an auditorium listening to a concert. Much of the sound we hear is *reflected sound,* meaning that it is bounced off the walls and ceiling, and comes to us from many directions.

Because sounds reach us from different angles, we hear the concert with both ears. We are able to tell, even with our eyes closed, that violins are playing on our left, because our left ear hears them slightly better than our right. The balance of sound we get from two-ear hearing—each ear hearing sounds slightly better from its own side—makes the music more exciting, clear, and complete. If you held a hand over one ear, you would see what a difference two-ear hearing makes. It would be like looking across the street, first with both eyes, and then with one eye closed. With both eyes, you have a more clear and complete picture. With both ears, you have a more clear and complete sound.

Stereophonic recording gives us the "two-ear listening experience" of the concert hall. This is how it is done.

As music is recorded, two groups of widely spaced microphones receive sounds from different angles. The sounds remain separate on the tape, from which the master record is made. Two sound channels are made in a single groove on the record you buy. The stylus picks up sounds from the different channels, and the cartridge sends them through two amplifiers in your record player. They go through two different loudspeaker systems, which send out two different sets of sound waves at the same time.

Our ears pick out the various sounds and instruments from the left and right. These are blended into a balanced, complete sound for a thrilling musical experience, very much like what we hear at the concert hall.

At one time, this new method of recording sound was known as *binaural,* meaning two-ear, recording. Stereo might be called an improved binaural method. Early binaural recordings were made with two closely spaced microphones. Stereo has a better, truer sound because groups

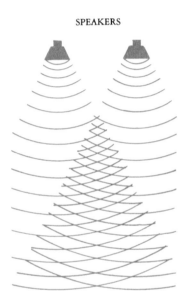

SPEAKERS

of microphones are used, and are more widely spaced.

"Two-ear" listening is a major improvement over *monaural,* or one-ear, recording. As you have seen, there are two channels of sound with stereo (and binaural). In monaural recording, there is no separation of sounds. Everything comes from one channel or one direction. It is like the example of holding a hand over one ear in the concert hall.

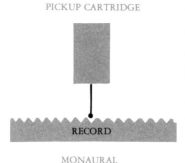

PICKUP CARTRIDGE

RECORD

MONAURAL

A monaural recording can still be a high fidelity recording. High fidelity, remember, refers to the sounds themselves, and not their direction. You can have high fidelity sound without having stereophonic sound. When you play back music that is both stereo *and* high fidelity, you have the most enjoyable sound possible today.

Stereophonic comes from two Greek words meaning "solid" and "sound". When we talk about records or tapes, it means "truth in sound" rather than "solid sound". This does not mean that high fidelity stereophonic recording is the final "truth" in sound. Scientists are always working on even newer and better ways of recording sound.

PICKUP CARTRIDGE

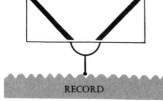

RECORD

STEREOPHONIC

This Is Progress

We have come a long way from the time when only a few hundred, and then only a few thousand people could hear music at one time. We have come a long way from Edison's first tin foil phonograph, from the old recording horn, and from old-fashioned 78 RPM records that played only about four minutes.

Every step forward in the development of recording devices has led to another step forward and to greater enjoyment of good music. This is true with high fidelity stereophonic sound. We know this is progress, and we are the ones to benefit. For music, remember, is for us, the listeners.

40

ABOUT THE AUTHOR

Robert K. Krishef says he was "about 10 years old" when he wrote his first short story. He has been deeply interested and involved in writing ever since. Mr. Krishef, born and raised in Minneapolis, is an experienced journalist who holds Bachelor's and Master's degrees in Journalism from the University of Minnesota. A former newspaperman and free lance writer, Mr. Krishef has been a reporter, sports editor and city editor on both daily and weekly newspapers and has written fiction and articles for various magazines. Presently he is director of public relations for an advertising agency which has as one of its clients a manufacturer of playback equipment. He is married, and Minneapolis is still his home.

41

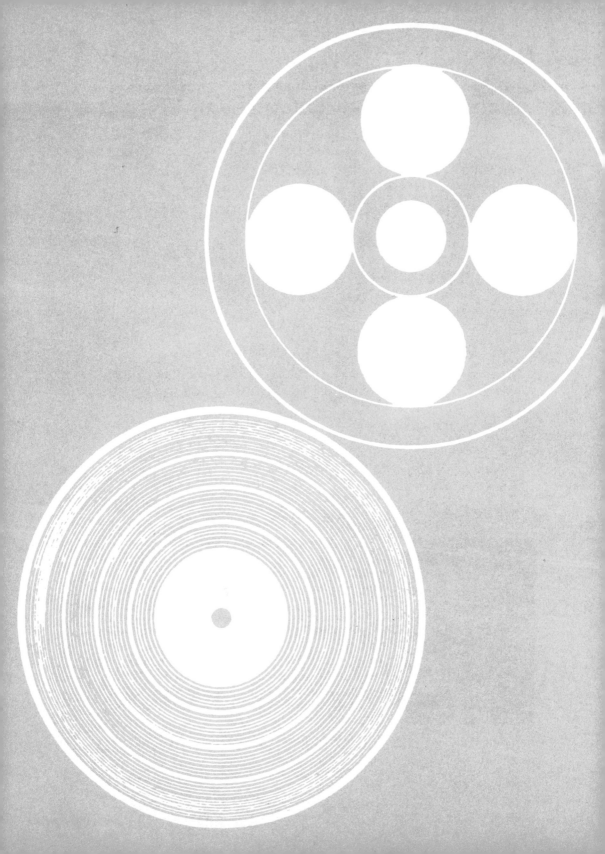

We specialize in publishing quality books for
young people. For a complete list please write

LERNER PUBLICATIONS COMPANY

241 First Avenue North, Minneapolis, Minnesota 55401